Awesome French Toast recipes

Explore to the delicious dessert cookbook ever!

Table of Contents

Introduction

What for breakfast, brunch, or your upcoming guests? Don't you have any idea what to cook after a day full of a busy schedule? I got you, and you will adore this French toast cookbook. It's packed with 30 different French toast flavors that even the pieces eater will enjoy every taste shown here. If you want a perfect presentation, you can serve the whole plate with fresh fruits and some sprigs of mint. Take a photo and share it on Instagram.

I am sure your post will become popular, and you will get a lot of attention on social media. Grab this book, and you will thank me later for how easy French Toast making can be.

1. Classic French Toast

Enrich your breakfast with this unique and classic French toast recipe that is always amazing to share with family and friends.

Servings: 4

Time: 30 minutes

The list of ingredients:

- 4 large eggs (room temperature)
- 1/4 cup whole milk
- 1/2 teaspoon vanilla extract

- 2 tablespoons granulated sugar
- 4 tablespoons butter
- 8 slices of brioche bread

Methods:

A. First, place in a large mixing bowl the eggs, whole milk, and vanilla extract.
B. Stir until everything is combined with the help of a wire whisk.
C. Stir in the granulated sugar and dip each brioche bread in the milk mixture.
D. Let everything soak well and fry the bread slices in a frying pan over medium heat with some butter.
E. Cook on both sides for about 2-3 minutes and enjoy with a drizzle of honey or maple syrup.

2. Cinnamon French Toast

If you adore my classic French toast recipe, adding a little bit of ground cinnamon to the egg and milk mixture will infuse your breakfast even more.

Servings: 4

Time: 30 minutes

The list of ingredients:

- 4 large eggs (room temperature)
- 1/4 cup whole milk
- 1/2 teaspoon vanilla extract

- 2 tablespoons granulated sugar
- 1 teaspoon ground cinnamon
- 4 tablespoons butter
- 8 slices of brioche bread

Methods:

A. First, place the eggs, whole milk, ground cinnamon, and vanilla extract in a large mixing bowl.

B. Stir until everything is combined with the help of a wire whisk.

C. Stir in the granulated sugar and dip each brioche bread in the milk mixture.

D. Let everything soak well and fry the bread slices in a frying pan over medium heat with some butter.

E. Cook on both sides for about 2-3 minutes and enjoy with a drizzle of honey or maple syrup.

3. Nutmeg French Toast

Nutmeg is a spice that infuses your meal with its fragrance and delicious taste.

Servings: 4

Time: 30 minutes

The list of ingredients:

- 4 large eggs (room temperature)
- 1/4 cup whole milk
- 1/2 teaspoon vanilla extract
- 2 tablespoons granulated sugar

- 1 teaspoon ground nutmeg
- 4 tablespoons butter
- 8 slices of brioche bread

Methods:

A. First, place the eggs, whole milk, ground nutmeg, and vanilla extract in a large mixing bowl.
B. Stir until everything is combined with the help of a wire whisk.
C. Stir in the granulated sugar and dip each brioche bread in the milk mixture.
D. Let everything soak well and fry the bread slices in a frying pan over medium heat with some butter.
E. Cook on both sides for about 2-3 minutes and enjoy with a drizzle of honey or maple syrup.

4. Rum French Toast

Adding some dark rum or rum extract will empower your French toast recipe and bring so much flavor.

Servings: 4

Time: 30 minutes

The list of ingredients:

- 4 large eggs (room temperature)
- 1/4 cup whole milk
- 1/2 teaspoon vanilla extract
- 2 tablespoons granulated sugar

- 1 teaspoon rum extract
- 4 tablespoons butter
- 8 slices of brioche bread

Methods:

A. First, place the eggs, whole milk, rum extract, and vanilla extract in a large mixing bowl.
B. Stir until everything is combined with the help of a wire whisk.
C. Stir in the granulated sugar and dip each brioche bread in the milk mixture.
D. Let everything soak well and fry the bread slices in a frying pan over medium heat with some butter.
E. Cook on both sides for about 2-3 minutes and enjoy with a drizzle of honey or maple syrup.

5. Almond French Toast

Adding some almond extract to your French toast batter will bring a flavor that's worth remembering.

Servings: 4

Time: 30 minutes

The list of ingredients:

- 4 large eggs (room temperature)
- 1/4 cup whole milk
- 1/2 teaspoon vanilla extract
- 2 tablespoons granulated sugar

- 1 teaspoon almond extract
- 4 tablespoons butter
- 8 slices of brioche bread

Methods:

A. First, place the eggs, whole milk, almond extract, and vanilla extract in a large mixing bowl.

B. Stir until everything is combined with the help of a wire whisk.

C. Stir in the granulated sugar and dip each brioche bread in the milk mixture.

D. Let everything soak well and fry the bread slices in a frying pan over medium heat with some butter.

E. Cook on both sides for about 2-3 minutes and enjoy with a drizzle of honey or maple syrup.

6. Coconut French Toast

Some coconut flakes will empower your breakfast with fantastic taste and rich flavor. This coconut-inspired French toast is an absolute favorite in our home.

Servings: 4

Time: 30 minutes

The list of ingredients:

- 4 large eggs (room temperature)
- 1/4 cup whole milk
- 1/2 teaspoon vanilla extract

- 2 tablespoons granulated sugar
- 2 tablespoons coconut flakes
- 4 tablespoons butter
- 8 slices of brioche bread

Methods:

A. First, place the eggs, whole milk, coconut flakes, and vanilla extract in a large mixing bowl.
B. Stir until everything is combined with the help of a wire whisk.
C. Stir in the granulated sugar and dip each brioche bread in the milk mixture.
D. Let everything soak well and fry the bread slices in a frying pan over medium heat with some butter.
E. Cook on both sides for about 2-3 minutes and enjoy with a drizzle of honey or maple syrup.

7. Honey French Toast

Sweeten up your next batch of French toast with the fantastic honey flavor. It's perfect for anyone who loves honey.

Servings: 4

Time: 30 minutes

The list of ingredients:

- 4 large eggs (room temperature)
- 1/4 cup whole milk
- 1/2 teaspoon vanilla extract
- 2 tablespoons granulated sugar

- 1 tablespoon honey
- 4 tablespoons butter
- 8 slices of brioche bread

Methods:

A. First, place the eggs, whole milk, honey, and vanilla extract in a large mixing bowl.

B. Stir until everything is combined with the help of a wire whisk.

C. Stir in the granulated sugar and dip each brioche bread in the milk mixture.

D. Let everything soak well and fry the bread slices in a frying pan over medium heat with some butter.

E. Cook on both sides for about 2-3 minutes and enjoy with a drizzle of honey or maple syrup.

8. Maple syrup French Toast

Did you know that maple syrup is a perfect and low-calorie sweetener? Not only that, but did you know that it will bring rich and delicious flavor to your French toast?

Servings: 4

Time: 30 minutes

The list of ingredients:

- 4 large eggs (room temperature)
- 1/4 cup whole milk
- 1/2 teaspoon vanilla extract

- 2 tablespoons granulated sugar
- 1 tablespoon maple syrup
- 4 tablespoons butter
- 8 slices of brioche bread

Methods:

A. First, place the eggs, whole milk, maple syrup, and vanilla extract in a large mixing bowl.

B. Stir until everything is combined with the help of a wire whisk.

C. Stir in the granulated sugar and dip each brioche bread in the milk mixture.

D. Let everything soak well and fry the bread slices in a frying pan over medium heat with some butter.

E. Cook on both sides for about 2-3 minutes and enjoy with a drizzle of honey or maple syrup.

9. Lemon French Toast

Lemon juice or lemon zest will bring a refreshing and robust citrus flavor that will amaze everyone with every bite.

Servings: 4

Time: 30 minutes

The list of ingredients:

- 4 large eggs (room temperature)
- 1/4 cup whole milk
- 1/2 teaspoon vanilla extract
- 2 tablespoons granulated sugar

- 1/2 lemon zest
- 4 tablespoons butter
- 8 slices of brioche bread

Methods:

A. First, place the eggs, whole milk, lemon zest, and vanilla extract in a large mixing bowl.

B. Stir until everything is combined with the help of a wire whisk.

C. Stir in the granulated sugar and dip each brioche bread in the milk mixture.

D. Let everything soak well and fry the bread slices in a frying pan over medium heat with some butter.

E. Cook on both sides for about 2-3 minutes and enjoy with a drizzle of honey or maple syrup.

10. Orange French Toast

Every French toast needs to be light, fluffy, and with the right refreshing taste. This orange flavor is a final try if you want an extra refreshing taste.

Servings: 4

Time: 30 minutes

The list of ingredients:

- 4 large eggs (room temperature)
- 1/4 cup whole milk
- 1/2 teaspoon vanilla extract

- 2 tablespoons granulated sugar

- 1/2 orange zest

- 4 tablespoons butter

- 8 slices of brioche bread

Methods:

A. First, place the eggs, whole milk, orange zest, and vanilla extract in a large mixing bowl.

B. Stir until everything is combined with the help of a wire whisk.

C. Stir in the granulated sugar and dip each brioche bread in the milk mixture.

D. Let everything soak well and fry the bread slices in a frying pan over medium heat with some butter.

E. Cook on both sides for about 2-3 minutes and enjoy with a drizzle of honey or maple syrup.

11. Lime French Toast

Fresh lime juice or zest will empower the French toast batter with a fantastic taste and refreshing flavor. You are going to adore this lime-inspired French toast recipe.

Servings: 4

Time: 30 minutes

The list of ingredients:

- 4 large eggs (room temperature)
- 1/4 cup whole milk
- 1/2 teaspoon vanilla extract

- 2 tablespoons granulated sugar
- 1/2 lime zest
- 4 tablespoons butter
- 8 slices of brioche bread

Methods:

A. First, place the eggs, whole milk, lime zest, and vanilla extract in a large mixing bowl.
B. Stir until everything is combined with the help of a wire whisk.
C. Stir in the granulated sugar and dip each brioche bread in the milk mixture.
D. Let everything soak well and fry the bread slices in a frying pan over medium heat with some butter.
E. Cook on both sides for about 2-3 minutes and enjoy with a drizzle of honey or maple syrup.

12. Chocolate French Toast

Chocolate French toast can be made using chocolate brioche bread, but why don't you add some cocoa powder and enjoy the flavor?

Servings: 4

Time: 30 minutes

The list of ingredients:

- 4 large eggs (room temperature)
- 1/4 cup whole milk
- 1/2 teaspoon vanilla extract

- 2 tablespoons granulated sugar
- 1 tablespoon cocoa powder
- 4 tablespoons butter
- 8 slices of brioche bread

Methods:

A. First, place the eggs, whole milk, cocoa powder, and vanilla extract in a large mixing bowl.
B. Stir until everything is combined with the help of a wire whisk.
C. Stir in the granulated sugar and dip each brioche bread in the milk mixture.
D. Let everything soak well and fry the bread slices in a frying pan over medium heat with some butter.
E. Cook on both sides for about 2-3 minutes and enjoy with a drizzle of honey or maple syrup.

13. Pumpkin French Toast

Adding some pumpkin puree to your French toast batter will make you feel the best fall flavor you have tasted.

Servings: 4

Time: 30 minutes

The list of ingredients:

- 4 large eggs (room temperature)
- 1/4 cup whole milk
- 1/2 teaspoon vanilla extract
- 2 tablespoons granulated sugar

- 1/4 cup pumpkin puree
- 4 tablespoons butter
- 8 slices of brioche bread

Methods:

A. First, place the eggs, whole milk, pumpkin puree, and vanilla extract in a large mixing bowl.

B. Stir until everything is combined with the help of a wire whisk.

C. Stir in the granulated sugar and dip each brioche bread in the milk mixture.

D. Let everything soak well and fry the bread slices in a frying pan over medium heat with some butter.

E. Cook on both sides for about 2-3 minutes and enjoy with a drizzle of honey or maple syrup.

14. Apple French Toast

In this recipe, you can use mashed cooked apple to get the puree or apple sauce for even better results and smoother texture.

Servings: 4

Time: 30 minutes

The list of ingredients:

- 4 large eggs (room temperature)
- 1/4 cup whole milk
- 1/2 teaspoon vanilla extract

- 2 tablespoons granulated sugar
- 1/4 cup apple sauce
- 4 tablespoons butter
- 8 slices of brioche bread

Methods:

A. First, place the eggs, whole milk, apple sauce, and vanilla extract in a large mixing bowl.
B. Stir until everything is combined with the help of a wire whisk.
C. Stir in the granulated sugar and dip each brioche bread in the milk mixture.
D. Let everything soak well and fry the bread slices in a frying pan over medium heat with some butter.
E. Cook on both sides for about 2-3 minutes and enjoy with a drizzle of honey or maple syrup.

15. Strawberry jam French Toast

If you want your French toast recipe to be different from the others than you should give this recipe a try.

Servings: 4

Time: 30 minutes

The list of ingredients:

- 4 large eggs (room temperature)
- 1/4 cup whole milk
- 1/2 teaspoon vanilla extract
- 2 tablespoons granulated sugar

- 4 tablespoons butter

- 8 slices of brioche bread

- 4 tablespoons strawberry jam

Methods:

A. First, place the eggs, whole milk, and vanilla extract in a large mixing bowl.

B. Stir until everything is combined with the help of a wire whisk.

C. Stir in the granulated sugar and dip each brioche bread in the milk mixture.

D. Let everything soak well and fry the bread slices in a frying pan over medium heat with some butter.

E. Cook on both sides for about 2-3 minutes and serve with some strawberry jam.

16. Apricot jam French Toast

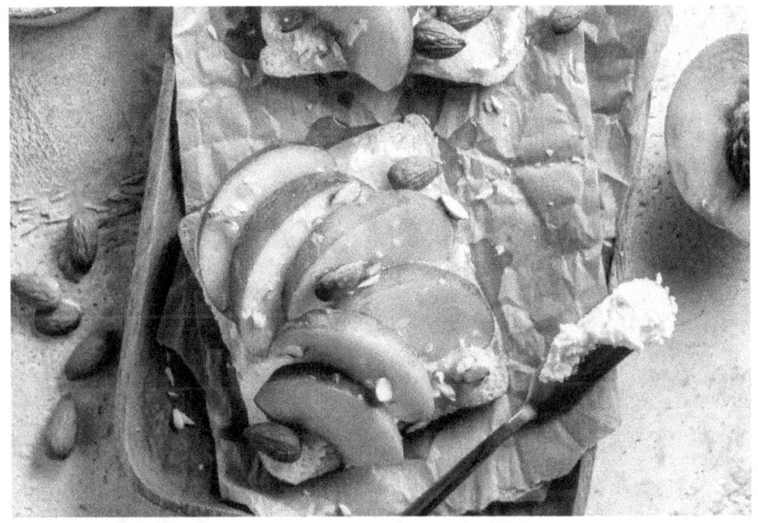

Apricot jam is very delicious, especially if it's homemade. Storebought will work fine in this recipe because you will serve your French toast with some apricot jam.

Servings: 4

Time: 30 minutes

The list of ingredients:

- 4 large eggs (room temperature)
- 1/4 cup whole milk
- 1/2 teaspoon vanilla extract

- 2 tablespoons granulated sugar
- 4 tablespoons butter
- 8 slices of brioche bread
- 4 tablespoons apricot jam

Methods:

A. First, place the eggs, whole milk, and vanilla extract in a large mixing bowl.
B. Stir until everything is combined with the help of a wire whisk.
C. Stir in the granulated sugar and dip each brioche bread in the milk mixture.
D. Let everything soak well and fry the bread slices in a frying pan over medium heat with some butter.
E. Cook on both sides for about 2-3 minutes and serve with some apricot jam.

17. Blueberry jam French Toast

I love blueberry jam with everything, including these fantastic French toast recipes. It's decadent and full of flavor.

Servings: 4

Time: 30 minutes

The list of ingredients:

- 4 large eggs (room temperature)
- 1/4 cup whole milk
- 1/2 teaspoon vanilla extract

- 2 tablespoons granulated sugar
- 4 tablespoons butter
- 8 slices of brioche bread
- 4 tablespoons blueberry jam

Methods:

A. First, place the eggs, whole milk, and vanilla extract in a large mixing bowl.
B. Stir until everything is combined with the help of a wire whisk.
C. Stir in the granulated sugar and dip each brioche bread in the milk mixture.
D. Let everything soak well and fry the bread slices in a frying pan over medium heat with some butter.
E. Cook on both sides for about 2-3 minutes and serve with some blueberry jam.

18. Raspberry jam French Toast

Raspberry jam is perfect for this recipe. Please make sure to get the raspberry jam without seeds because you will enjoy a smooth and rich raspberry experience.

Servings: 4

Time: 30 minutes

The list of ingredients:

- 4 large eggs (room temperature)
- 1/4 cup whole milk
- 1/2 teaspoon vanilla extract

- 2 tablespoons granulated sugar
- 4 tablespoons butter
- 8 slices of brioche bread
- 4 tablespoons raspberry jam

Methods:

A. First, place the eggs, whole milk, and vanilla extract in a large mixing bowl.

B. Stir until everything is combined with the help of a wire whisk.

C. Stir in the granulated sugar and dip each brioche bread in the milk mixture.

D. Let everything soak well and fry the bread slices in a frying pan over medium heat with some butter.

E. Cook on both sides for about 2-3 minutes and serve with some raspberry jam.

19. Currant jam French Toast

Black or red currant jam is perfect for this recipe. The rich and delicious flavor from the jam will infuse the fried French dough. This recipe goes well with some butter.

Servings: 4

Time: 30 minutes

The list of ingredients:

- 4 large eggs (room temperature)
- 1/4 cup whole milk
- 1/2 teaspoon vanilla extract

- 2 tablespoons granulated sugar
- 4 tablespoons butter
- 8 slices of brioche bread
- 4 tablespoons black currant jam

Methods:

A. First, place the eggs, whole milk, and vanilla extract in a large mixing bowl.
B. Stir until everything is combined with the help of a wire whisk.
C. Stir in the granulated sugar and dip each brioche bread in the milk mixture.
D. Let everything soak well and fry the bread slices in a frying pan over medium heat with some butter.
E. Cook on both sides for about 2-3 minutes and serve with black currant jam.

20 .Peanut butter French Toast

Adding some peanut butter to your French toast is so gorgeous. The peanut butter will slowly melt on a warm piece of French toast. Yum!

Servings: 4

Time: 30 minutes

The list of ingredients:

- 4 large eggs (room temperature)
- 1/4 cup whole milk
- 1/2 teaspoon vanilla extract

- 2 tablespoons granulated sugar
- 4 tablespoons butter
- 8 slices of brioche bread
- 4 tablespoons peanut butter

Methods:

A. First, place the eggs, whole milk, and vanilla extract in a large mixing bowl.

B. Stir until everything is combined with the help of a wire whisk.

C. Stir in the granulated sugar and dip each brioche bread in the milk mixture.

D. Let everything soak well and fry the bread slices in a frying pan over medium heat with some butter.

E. Cook on both sides for about 2-3 minutes and serve with peanut butter.

21. Almond butter French Toast

Almond butter is an excellent source of protein and a delicious way to start your morning. Imagine a warm piece of French toast spread with some almond butter. Delicious!

Servings: 4

Time: 30 minutes

The list of ingredients:

- 4 large eggs (room temperature)
- 1/4 cup whole milk
- 1/2 teaspoon vanilla extract

- 2 tablespoons granulated sugar
- 4 tablespoons butter
- 8 slices of brioche bread
- 4 tablespoons almond butter

Methods:

A. First, place the eggs, whole milk, and vanilla extract in a large mixing bowl.

B. Stir until everything is combined with the help of a wire whisk.

C. Stir in the granulated sugar and dip each brioche bread in the milk mixture.

D. Let everything soak well and fry the bread slices in a frying pan over medium heat with some butter.

E. Cook on both sides for about 2-3 minutes and serve with almond butter.

22. Hazelnut butter French Toast

Spread some hazelnut butter and enjoy the flavors in your mouth. It's going to be a party for your taste buds.

Servings: 4

Time: 30 minutes

The list of ingredients:

- 4 large eggs (room temperature)
- 1/4 cup whole milk
- 1/2 teaspoon vanilla extract
- 2 tablespoons granulated sugar

- 4 tablespoons butter
- 8 slices of brioche bread
- 4 tablespoons hazelnut butter

Methods:

A. First, place the eggs, whole milk, and vanilla extract in a large mixing bowl.

B. Stir until everything is combined with the help of a wire whisk.

C. Stir in the granulated sugar and dip each brioche bread in the milk mixture.

D. Let everything soak well and fry the bread slices in a frying pan over medium heat with some butter.

E. Cook on both sides for about 2-3 minutes and serve with hazelnut butter.

23. Peanut butter and chocolate chips French Toast

Did you know that peanut butter and chocolate chips are one of the greatest flavor combinations? Now you do, and don't forget to try this recipe because it's oh my GOD!

Servings: 4

Time: 30 minutes

The list of ingredients:

- 4 large eggs (room temperature)
- 1/4 cup whole milk

- 1/2 teaspoon vanilla extract
- 2 tablespoons granulated sugar
- 4 tablespoons butter
- 8 slices of brioche bread
- 4 tablespoons peanut butter
- 1/4 cup mini chocolate chips

Methods:

A. First, place the eggs, whole milk, and vanilla extract in a large mixing bowl.
B. Stir until everything is combined with the help of a wire whisk.
C. Stir in the granulated sugar and dip each brioche bread in the milk mixture.
D. Let everything soak well and fry the bread slices in a frying pan over medium heat with some butter.
E. Cook on both sides for about 2-3 minutes and serve with peanut butter and mini chocolate chips.

24. Nutella French Toast

We all love Nutella, but what if we add some Nutella to a warm piece of French toast for a rich and decadent breakfast?

Servings: 4

Time: 30 minutes

The list of ingredients:

- 4 large eggs (room temperature)
- 1/4 cup whole milk
- 1/2 teaspoon vanilla extract

- 2 tablespoons granulated sugar
- 4 tablespoons butter
- 8 slices of brioche bread
- 4 tablespoons Nutella

Methods:

A. First, place the eggs, whole milk, and vanilla extract in a large mixing bowl.
B. Stir until everything is combined with the help of a wire whisk.
C. Stir in the granulated sugar and dip each brioche bread in the milk mixture.
D. Let everything soak well and fry the bread slices in a frying pan over medium heat with some butter.
E. Cook on both sides for about 2-3 minutes and serve with Nutella.

25. Peanut butter and jam French Toast

Did you know that peanut butter is perfect for any jam? My favoruite is peanut butter and strawberry jam, but you can pick your flavor.

Servings: 4

Time: 30 minutes

The list of ingredients:

- 4 large eggs (room temperature)
- 1/4 cup whole milk

- 1/2 teaspoon vanilla extract

- 2 tablespoons granulated sugar

- 4 tablespoons butter

- 8 slices of brioche bread

- 4 tablespoons peanut butter

- 4 tablespoons strawberry jam

Methods:

A. First, place the eggs, whole milk, and vanilla extract in a large mixing bowl.

B. Stir until everything is combined with the help of a wire whisk.

C. Stir in the granulated sugar and dip each brioche bread in the milk mixture.

D. Let everything soak well and fry the bread slices in a frying pan over medium heat with some butter.

E. Cook on both sides for about 2-3 minutes and serve with peanut butter and strawberry jam.

26. Powdered sugar French Toast

One of the classic ways to enjoy a simple French toast recipe is to dust it with a bit of powdered sugar on top.

Servings: 4

Time: 30 minutes

The list of ingredients:

- 4 large eggs (room temperature)
- 1/4 cup whole milk
- 1/2 teaspoon vanilla extract
- 2 tablespoons granulated sugar

- 4 tablespoons butter

- 8 slices of brioche bread

- 4 tablespoons powdered sugar

Methods:

A. First, place the eggs, whole milk, and vanilla extract in a large mixing bowl.

B. Stir until everything is combined with the help of a wire whisk.

C. Stir in the granulated sugar and dip each brioche bread in the milk mixture.

D. Let everything soak well and fry the bread slices in a frying pan over medium heat with some butter.

E. Cook on both sides for about 2-3 minutes and serve with powdered sugar.

27. Blueberry jam and lemon French Toast

When serving your French toast recipe with blueberry jam, just add some lemon zest and enjoy this fantastic flavor.

Servings: 4

Time: 30 minutes

The list of ingredients:

- 4 large eggs (room temperature)
- 1/4 cup whole milk
- 1/2 teaspoon vanilla extract

- 2 tablespoons granulated sugar
- 4 tablespoons butter
- 8 slices of brioche bread
- 4 tablespoons blueberry jam
- 1/2 lemon zest

Methods:

A. First, place the eggs, whole milk, and vanilla extract in a large mixing bowl.

B. Stir until everything is combined with the help of a wire whisk.

C. Stir in the granulated sugar and dip each brioche bread in the milk mixture.

D. Let everything soak well and fry the bread slices in a frying pan over medium heat with some butter.

E. Cook on both sides for about 2-3 minutes and serve with blueberry jam and lemon zest.

28. Raspberry jam and chocolate chips French Toast

Adding some chocolate chips to your French toast with raspberry jam will bring delicious flavor and a unique taste.

Servings: 4

Time: 30 minutes

The list of ingredients:

- 4 large eggs (room temperature)
- 1/4 cup whole milk
- 1/2 teaspoon vanilla extract

- 2 tablespoons granulated sugar

- 4 tablespoons butter

- 8 slices of brioche bread

- 4 tablespoons raspberry jam

- 1/4 cup chocolate chips

Methods:

A. First, place the eggs, whole milk, and vanilla extract in a large mixing bowl.

B. Stir until everything is combined with the help of a wire whisk.

C. Stir in the granulated sugar and dip each brioche bread in the milk mixture.

D. Let everything soak well and fry the bread slices in a frying pan over medium heat with some butter.

E. Cook on both sides for about 2-3 minutes and serve with raspberry jam and chocolate chips.

29. Honey and Cinnamon French Toast

Drizzle your French toast with honey and sprinkle some cinnamon for a more decadent presentation and taste.

Servings: 4

Time: 30 minutes

The list of ingredients:

- 4 large eggs (room temperature)
- 1/4 cup whole milk
- 1/2 teaspoon vanilla extract

- 2 tablespoons granulated sugar
- 4 tablespoons butter
- 8 slices of brioche bread
- 4 tablespoons honey
- 1 teaspoon ground cinnamon

Methods:

A. First, place the eggs, whole milk, and vanilla extract in a large mixing bowl.
B. Stir until everything is combined with the help of a wire whisk.
C. Stir in the granulated sugar and dip each brioche bread in the milk mixture.
D. Let everything soak well and fry the bread slices in a frying pan over medium heat with some butter.
E. Cook on both sides for about 2-3 minutes and serve with honey and ground cinnamon.

30. Black currant jam French Toast

Did you know that black currant jam is perfect for pancakes and French toast? Its unique, pungent flavor is fantastic for this kind of dessert.

Servings: 4

Time: 30 minutes

The list of ingredients:

- 4 large eggs (room temperature)
- 1/4 cup whole milk
- 1/2 teaspoon vanilla extract

- 2 tablespoons granulated sugar
- 4 tablespoons butter
- 8 slices of brioche bread
- 4 tablespoons black currant jam

Methods:

A. First, place the eggs, whole milk, and vanilla extract in a large mixing bowl.
B. Stir until everything is combined with the help of a wire whisk.
C. Stir in the granulated sugar and dip each brioche bread in the milk mixture.
D. Let everything soak well and fry the bread slices in a frying pan over medium heat with some butter.
E. Cook on both sides for about 2-3 minutes and serve with black currant jam.

Conclusion

Having French toast for breakfast is the best way to enjoy delicious meal at the beginning of the day. Your French toast can be loaded with ton of fresh fruits and different toppings such as honey, maple syrup, marshmallows or even chocolate chips.

This book is packed with 30 different flavors of this amazing meal, and you will have a month full of different tastes and feast for your tastebuds.

Be sure to have some eggs, toast bread and some milk in order to make the best French toast in the world. Each and every flavor will help you taste one of the best possible flavor combinations.